CREATIVE BASKET WEAVING

Sylvie Bégot

CREATIVE BASKET WEAVING

Step-by-Step Instructions for Gathering and Drying, Braiding, Weaving, and Projects

STACKPOLE
BOOKS

Guilford, Connecticut

Published by Stackpole Books
An imprint of The Rowman & Littlefield Publishing Group, Inc.
4501 Forbes Blvd., Ste. 200
Lanham, MD 20706
www.stackpolebooks.com

Distributed by NATIONAL BOOK NETWORK
800-462-6420

Original French title: *Vannerie nature*
Copyright © 2018 Éditions Eyrolles, Paris, France

Graphic design: Sophie Charbonnel
Adaptation of mock-up and layout: Anne Krawczyk
Background photos: Camille Riglet
All photos in the Tools, Materials & Techniques section and the step-by-step
project photos are those of the author.
Translation: Nancy Gingrich, Mithril Translations

British Library Cataloguing in Publication Information available

Library of Congress Cataloging-in-Publication Data available

Names: Bégot, Sylvie, author.
Title: Creative basket weaving : step-by-step instructions for gathering and
    drying, braiding, weaving, and projects / Sylvie Bégot ; translation: Nancy
    Gingrich, Mithril Translations.
Other titles: Vannerie nature. English
Description: First edition. | Lanham, MD : Stackpole Books, an imprint of
    Rowman & Littlefield Publishing Group, [2020] | Translation of: Vannerie
    nature. | Summary: "So many interesting basketry designs can be made
    from plant leaves and bark that you can find in nature or purchase from
    suppliers. Learn how to harvest these materials and use the basic
    materials and weaving techniques to make projects ranging from
    traditional baskets to wall hangings to a shoulder bag, pencil cup,
    Christmas decorations, and much more"— Provided by publisher.
Identifiers: LCCN 2020005394 (print) | LCCN 2020005395 (ebook) | ISBN
    9780811739177 (paper ; alk. paper) | ISBN 9780811769099 (electronic)
Subjects: LCSH: Basket making.
Classification: LCC TT879.B3 .B44313 2020 (print) | LCC TT879.B3 (ebook)
    | DDC 746.41—dc23
LC record available at https://lccn.loc.gov/2020005394
LC ebook record available at https://lccn.loc.gov/2020005395

First Edition

CONTENTS

INTRODUCTION

Nature is a constant source of inspiration, no matter the season. Spring in particular offers an immense palette of colors, and fall is rich in unexpected treasures! These two seasons give me the chance to collect all sorts of materials to indulge in my passion: basket weaving.

My superstars are dried iris leaves. They have inspired several creations that I use in my daily life. Sweet chestnut bark and willow bark also have a special place in my basket weaving, even if their use is not yet very widespread.

I have collected other treasures from numerous walks in different natural environments, such as shells and pierced stones, all sorts of pinecones, lichens, and so forth. I integrate them at whim when weaving my baskets.

Through this book, I hope to share with you the pleasure of making cordage and braiding and weaving with natural fibers collected in nature to make items that you can you use in your daily life.

A chapter is dedicated to each of the materials explored in these pages. The projects progress in difficulty through each chapter.

Making baskets from wild plants allows us to practice an ancient ancestral art, to learn to do for ourselves with our own hands, and to observe our environment in a different way. Be curious about the nature surrounding you—basket making will help you appreciate all of its magic.

TOOLS, MATERIALS, **AND** **TECHNIQUES**

Nature makes available to us a multitude of fibers with basket-weaving properties. Experimenting with them has led to the discovery of a variety of techniques. The following section explains the main techniques, as well as the tools and materials you will need to carry them out. Some techniques are suitable for several fibers. Cordage, for example, can be made with iris or cattail leaves, but also with other leaves that hold up to the twisting. Do some testing to adapt the techniques to the fibers found in your yard.

TOOLS AND MATERIALS

BASIC KIT

There are a few tools and materials you will want to keep close at hand. These will make up the basic kit for your basket-weaving station.

You will only need a few basic tools to make the various projects in this book:

- pruning shears to cut large branches
- snips to cut small ones
- an awl to spread apart the weaving to make it easier to pass other parts through
- a folding tool to mark the fibers and make them easier to bend
- a pruning knife to cut and bend the strips

- a utility knife for precisely cutting bark
- an Opinel-style knife to make notches on the willow sticks
- a metal ruler for taking precise measurements and to make cutting easier

To assemble the braids or fasten elements during basket weaving, you will also need:

- linen twine
- a large needle (such as a mattress or yarn needle)
- a pair of scissors
- clothespins

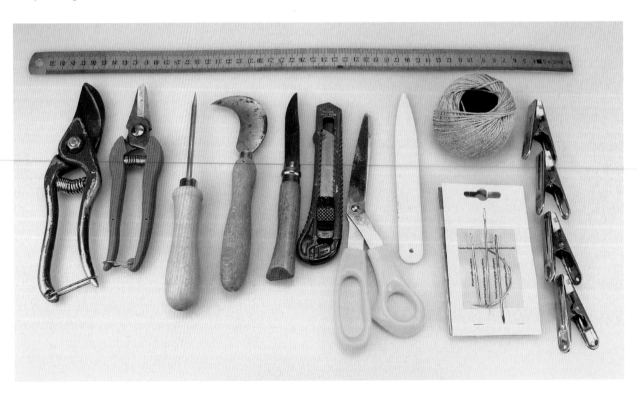

OTHER TOOLS

Some projects will need specific tools, such as a sewing machine (for the shoulder bag and the stool cover), a hot glue gun (for the double heart), a drill or gimlet (for the button on the shoulder bag, the bird feeder, and the basket), a staple gun (for the stool cover), and so forth. Take the time to read through the tools and materials needed before starting, and don't hesitate to use items you have on hand.

RAW MATERIALS

Cattail

This plant is often confused with reed or bulrush, as it grows in wet areas, usually with its roots in water. However, it belongs to the botanical family Typhaceae. It can be identified by its elongated brown flower head and its leaves, which can be 3–6 ft. (1–2 m) in length and ½–¾ in. (1.3–2 cm) wide for the most common type.

Cattail, found throughout North America, is gathered along the edge of ditches and rivers. To find it, simply be aware of how it looks and observe your surroundings.

Harvesting

Cattail can be harvested at the end of summer (end of August/beginning of September). The plant must be cut at the base with pruning shears.

Sort the leaves to remove those that have holes, are cut, or are too narrow. Cut off the spongy base, as it is not used for basket weaving.

Drying

Place the sorted leaves flat on an old sheet in a well-ventilated area away from any moisture so they can dry properly.

Once or twice a week, turn the leaves for uniform drying. Continue to do this until the leaves no longer smell like wet grass and are dry to the touch. This process will take approximately one month.

Ready to Use

Before starting a basket-weaving project using cattail leaves, you will only need to dip them in water briefly and then wrap in a damp cloth. After 20–30 minutes, the leaves will be ready to use.

Iris Leaves

A flowering iris is beautiful, which makes it a well-loved plant in the garden, and it's simple to grow. Your gardener friends will be happy to let you collect the dried leaves.

Harvesting

The leaves must be pulled up at their base by hand. If they don't pull off easily, stop trying and don't remove them, as you may harm the rhizome and compromise the plant's ability to flower the next year.

Storing

Place all the leaves in the same direction and wrap in bundles. Bind each bundle with a long iris leaf or some type of tie.

Drying

Place the wrapped bundles in an area free from moisture and adequately ventilated in order to complete the drying process. This process will take from one to two weeks.

Different varieties of iris will have leaves of distinct colors. Keep the varieties separate, and then you can easily select from the natural colors as you weave for desired effects.

Ready to Use
Before starting a basket-weaving project using iris leaves, dip them in water briefly and then wrap in a damp cloth. After 15 minutes, the leaves will be ready to use.

Bark

It is not very common to make baskets using bark, as this is not a traditional practice. I use willow, sweet chestnut, or hazel bark. These plants are more often used in other ways in basketry. Willow stems, which correspond to the new year's growth, are called "wicker." Wicker is used raw, with or without its bark. Wicker without its bark is called "white wicker." Chestnut is used in slats, and hazel in thin strips called "splints."

Varieties
Projects in this book using bark are mainly made with sweet chestnut, but you are free to use other types depending on the trees or shrubs found in your area, such as hazel, willow, mimosa, forsythia, and so forth.

Willow

GATHERING

Two different methods are used to remove willow bark, depending on the time of year.

In winter, starting in January, the method consists of cutting large, straight willow stems without offshoots, approximately ¾–1 in. (2–2.5 cm) in diameter. The stems are then wrapped in bundles and placed upright in a shallow, fairly wide container called a "retting tank," filled with 6 in. (15 cm) of water (a plastic washbasin or similar container will also work). This keeps the stems from drying out and allows them to start regrowth in the spring.

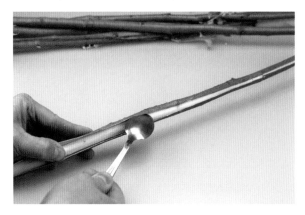

2. Carefully slide the backside of a small spoon along the cut to peel off the bark little by little.

The other possible period for harvesting is spring, when the plants begin to grow again and little leaves appear, from March to the end of June, depending on the region in which you live. Select and cut stems and branches that are straight and without any offshoots, approximately ¾–1 in. (2–2.5 cm) in diameter.

3. Peel off the base of the stem around the entire width.

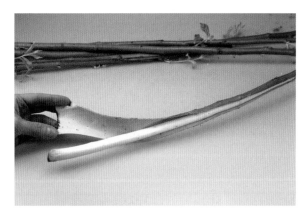

> **Note**
>
> If you harvest the willow stems in the spring, removal of the bark must take place within an hour of cutting the branch. If this is not possible, place the base of the cut branches in a container filled with 6 in. (15 cm) water.

REMOVAL OF BARK

1. Cut along the length of the stem with a utility knife or other pointed knife. Start at the top of the stem and end at its base.

4. Slowly roll up the bark that has been peeled off, with the wrong side facing you.

5. Use a piece of string to tie the bark in a roll.

6. Place the rolls of bark in a cardboard or wooden box (avoid plastic), and let them dry for two months.

Sweet Chestnut and Hazel

In the forest between May and June, you can saw off shoots one to two years old with a cut 1–2 in. (3–5 cm) in diameter.

1. Bring a wood saw, a utility or regular knife, and a small spoon.

2. Cut a 6 ft. (2 m) long section, and remove and roll the bark from the stem using the same method as for willow.

> **Recommendation**
>
> If you are in a private forest, ask the owner for permission to take sweet chestnut or hazel shoots. Only collect what you need.

Tie the bark in rolls, with the wrong side facing you, and leave them to dry all summer long.

Preparing Strips

Prepare strips just before starting on a basket-making project.

Let the bark strips soak in warm water for 30 minutes to 1 hour, depending on their thickness.

Get a cutting mat or an old calendar, a utility knife, a metal straight edge, or a ruler for use with a rotary cutter.

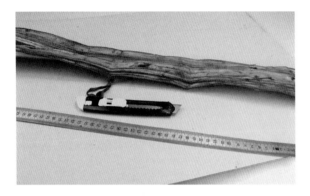

Carefully unroll the bark roll and make an even edge by cutting it along one side. Cut the strips to size according to what is needed for the project.

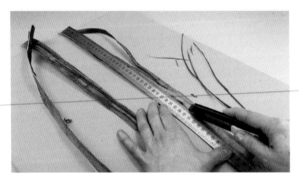

Combining Colors
Have fun playing with both sides of a piece of bark to vary the colors in your basket-making projects.

Willow (Wicker) Stems

Willow stems are cut at the base in winter starting in the month of January, during a waning moon, so they will stay in good condition when stored. They are subsequently sorted by height, then by diameter in a batch of the same height, and bundled together. The base of the stem is also called the "foot" and the thin end of the stem the "top."

Let them dry in a well-ventilated area away from the light.

Branches from Pruning Trees

The pruning of ornamental trees provides a good resource for branches of varying colors. The projects in this book suggest using straight branches from ornamental plum or cherry trees for their deep plum color.

Shoots from hazel trees, plane trees, and olive trees can also be used—the important thing is that the branches are thin and straight and have different colorings.

TECHNIQUES

TWO-STRAND CORDAGE (IRIS LEAVES)

Wetting the Leaves

1. Under the shower or a faucet, spray warm water on a handful of iris leaves and wrap them in a damp cloth for half an hour.

Cordage

2. Place two iris leaves together top to tail.

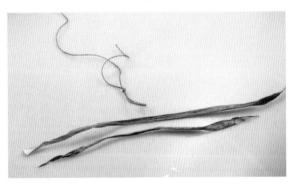

3. With a piece of linen twine, tie a loop around the middle of the leaves without tightening it. Attach the twine to a solid anchor point and fold the leaves in half.

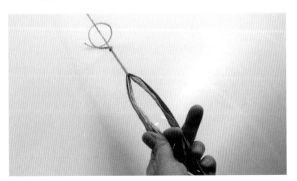

4. Hold one half of the bundle with each hand, between the thumb and index finger, and twist them in the same direction, keeping them consistently taut.

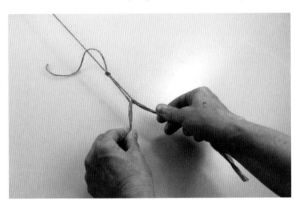

5. Pass the right side over the left, and continue in this manner to produce a reverse twist and lock it in place.

> **Note**
> Increase the number of leaves for a thicker cord.

Adding a New Leaf

6. When there are only 2 in. (5 cm) left at the end of one of the leaves, add in a new one.

7. Place the end of the new leaf on the longer strand and then continue twisting the shorter strand and the new leaf.

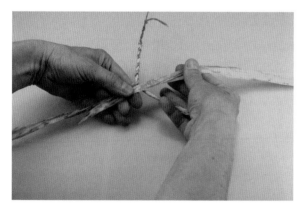

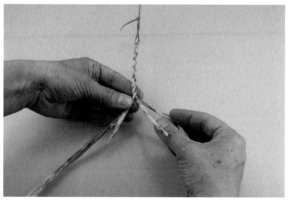

8. To put the cordage on hold to continue later, make a loop with the two strands of cord.

9. Using snips or scissors, cut off protruding ends where leaves were added.

10. Roll up the cordage to store it.

THREE-STRAND BRAID (IRIS LEAVES)

Braiding

1. Place six to seven leaves top to tail and tie the middle of the bundle with linen twine (the number of leaves in the bundle determines the thickness of the braid that will be made). Attach the twine to a solid anchor point to support the pull from the braiding.

2. Divide the leaves into three sections and start braiding.

3. Just as when braiding hair, hold the strands fairly taut to obtain a neat braid.

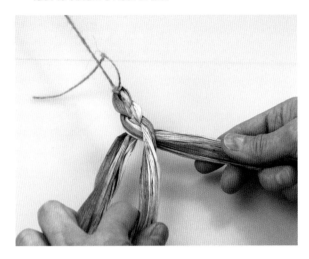

Adding a New Leaf

4. When the shortest section is in the middle, place the end of a new leaf under it and continue braiding.

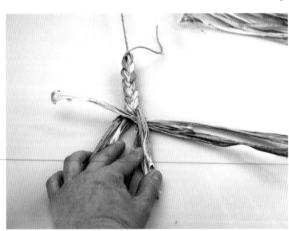

5. Continue to add new leaves as needed to keep the braid diameter consistent.

Finishing

6. When you have reached the desired length of braid, remove the twine and use scissors to cut the unwoven ends of the braid, as for cordage.

7. Roll up the braid to store.

RANDING (ALL FIBERS)

The simplest form of weaving in basket making is called randing. It consists of weaving over one stake, under one stake, over the next, and so on.

WOVEN BASE (CATTAIL LEAVES)

This base is the one that most resembles weaving. It simply consists of weaving a flat bottom that holds the cattail leaves in place to build up the basket.

Base

1. Select the thickest and widest cattail leaves. Put them together in pairs, one on top of the other top to tail.

2. On a flat work surface, place two pairs vertically and one pair horizontally. Weave the horizontal pair over and then under the vertical pairs.

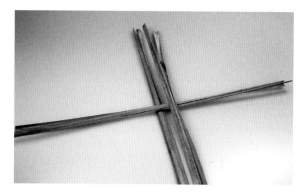

3. Add a second pair of horizontal leaves, reversing the weaving (under/over). The leaves must fit tightly next to one another. Lift them up if necessary to make it easier to weave and move them closer together.

4. Add horizontal and vertical pairs until reaching the desired size of the base.

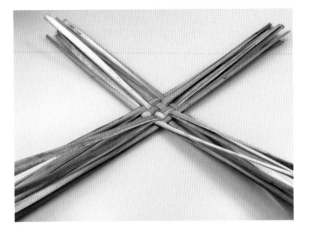

Weaving

5. Split a long cattail leaf in two and fold it in half. Place the loop thus formed around one pair of leaves in the left corner to weave from left to right (left-handers will place it in the right corner to weave from right to left).

6. Start twining (see explanation of this technique on p. 26) with the left strand (left-handers will use the one on the right). Weave by alternating each strand over and then under each pair.

7. Go all the way around the base in this manner to hold the weaving in place; then keep the strands on hold.

HOW TO END WEAVING

When changing weaving techniques, it is important to securely attach the previous ends.

1. Thread the last strand woven into a mattress needle, insert under the weaving, and bring up on the right side in the third previous row.

2. Use scissors to cut off protruding ends.

WOVEN BORDER

This final intertwining produces a firm and pretty edge on the basket.

1. Start opposite the point the weaving ended. Bend a spoke and pass it behind the next spoke, wedging a small wicker stick at its base.

2. Bend all the following spokes in the same way.

3. Remove the small wicker stick and slide the last spoke through the open space.

4. Split a thin cattail leaf in two; then fold it in half and place the loop formed around a spoke.

5. Twine two rounds (see explanation of this technique on p. 26).

6. Thread the last strand woven into a mattress needle, insert under the weaving, and bring up on the right side in the third previous row.

FOUR-STRAND BRAID (CATTAIL LEAVES)

1. To make weaving easier and limit drying shrinkage, place the cattail leaves in a rolling machine or flatten them with a rolling pin, going over them several times.

2. Bend a leaf into a V and slide a second leaf through the V horizontally.

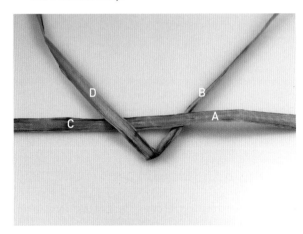

3. Fold strip A behind the leaf bent in the V-shape so that it ends up parallel to strip D.

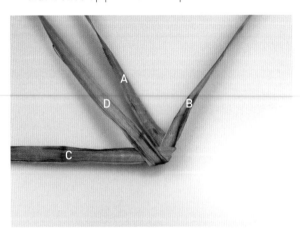

4. Fold strip C over strip D and then under strip A so that it ends up parallel to strip B.

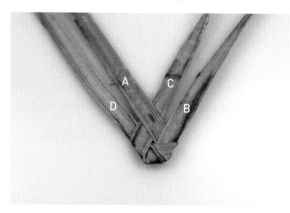

5. Continue to weave in the same manner, alternating the outside right and left strips.

How to Add a New Leaf

6. When there are 3 in. (8 cm) or less of leaf remaining, place the end of a new leaf on top of it (overlapping an inch or so), and then continue weaving, all while keeping the two ends overlapping.

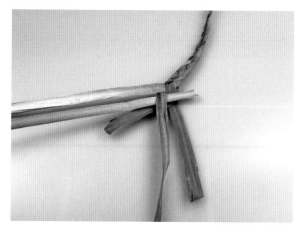

7. Braid to the desired length, pulling it taut from time to time to tighten up the braid.

Finishing

8. Wind in a wreath shape to store.

9. With scissors, cut off the ends of leaves protruding from the braid.

Tip
If you work on this task over several days, spray some water on the braid each time you start working on it again.

WEAVING TECHNIQUES (ALL FIBERS)

Basket weaving is like knitting in that there are numerous strokes (as there are stitches), or techniques, that can be used with all the materials used in this book.

Twining

Twining, also called pairing, is a fairly easy weave, and therefore you can become proficient at it quite quickly. It is worked with two weavers. The weavers used must be a smaller diameter than the spokes. (The photos show spokes set in a drilled piece of wood, but this is certainly not the only possible configuration.)

1. Bend a long weaver in half and place the fold behind a spoke.

2. Bring the left weaver in front of the first spoke, behind the second spoke, and then back out front. Inversely, the right weaver starts behind the first spoke and is brought over the front of the second spoke. Continue in this pattern with the two weavers, crossing them between spokes.

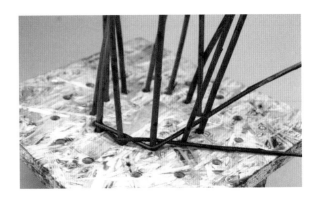

Adding New Weavers

3. Pull the foot (base of the stem) out in front of a spoke to make room to insert a new weaver behind it. The foot of this new weaver is then held in place behind the spoke in the same space as the end of the weaver.

4. Slide the top (tip of the stem) of the new weaver into the same space and under the first weaver. Weave with the two tips over 8 in. (20 cm).

5. To end weaving, simply place the weavers on the inside of the basket.

Triple Twining

Triple twining (or three-rod wale) is a stronger, denser weave than regular twining, and it gives a solid base to the basket. As for twining, this technique requires weavers that are a smaller diameter than the spokes. It is worked with three weavers.

1. To begin triple twining at the base of the basket, trim the foot of three weavers and insert them into the bottom, between two consecutive spokes.

2. Always start with the far left weaver. Bring it in front of the two spokes to the right, behind the next spoke and back out. Repeat this sequence with the two other weavers, weaving with the far left one each time.

3. To end, place the weavers inside the basket, each between different spokes.

Double Randing

The double randing weave (or two-rod slewing) is very decorative with the two weavers together.

1. Insert the foot of a weaver behind a spoke and begin by weaving in front of and behind the next two spokes. Add the second weaver behind the third spoke.

2. Continue weaving with the two weavers parallel. When you reach the tip of a weaver, place it inside the basket and insert the foot of a new weaver, continuing in the same pattern.

STAR BASE (BARK)

1. Place the strips one on top of each other and, in the center, nail them to a board. Fan the strips out into evenly spaced spokes.

2. On each strip, make a pencil mark 1½ in. (4 cm) out from the center.

> **Note**
>
> The distance from the center depends on the width of the strips: the wider the strips, the larger the radius.

3. Fold about 1 yd. (1 m) of linen twine in half and place the loop around one of the strips.

4. Start twining 1½ in. (4 cm) out from the center.

SEWN BORDER (BARK)

1. Place a strip inside your project, at the top of the weaving. Hold it in place with clothespins.

2. Cut a piece of linen twine that is three times the length of the circumference of the border and tie it to the strip placed inside. Bend the first strip of the border horizontally.

3. Place it behind the next strip. Fasten the bent strip with the twine by bringing it from the inside to the outside of the pot, between the strips.

4. Trim off the excess strip.

5. Continue in the same way around the entire circumference of the basket.

6. Cut the last strip and place it in the border. Tie firmly to finish off.

7. Remember to keep the twine taut as you are making the border.

SPIRAL WEAVING (WICKER)

Spiral weaving produces an even twist on each of the stems. This technique can be used to make wicker rattles.

1. Get five wicker stems about 30 in. (80 cm) long.

2. Securely tie the tips of the five stems together with string.

3. Spread open the bunch of stems and hold the tips in your left hand (right hand if you are left-handed).

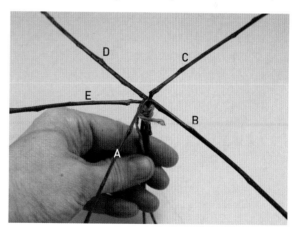

4. Start the spiral weaving. Place stem A over the next two stems (B and C) in a counterclockwise direction.

Then bring stem C over stems A and D, and continue in this pattern with the other stems.

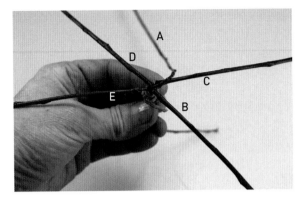

5. At the end of the first round, you have formed a square.

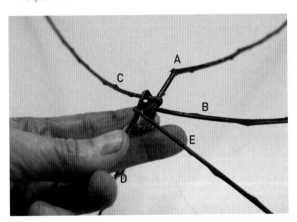

6. The spiral weave is composed of the same repetitive spiral movement. To widen the shape, place stem A over stem B and parallel to stem C.

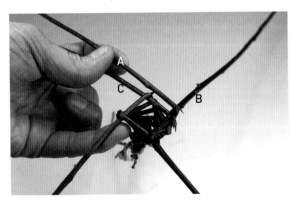

7. Bring stem C back over A and position it parallel to stem D.

8. Continue in this pattern for the whole length of the stems. To finish up, lock the spiral weave by sliding the shortest end under stem E.

Last stem locked in.

JAPANESE KNOT (WICKER)

This decorative knot can be used to hold a bundle of fibers together.

1. To make this knot with a wicker stem, insert the foot of the stem in the center of a bundle and perpendicular to it.

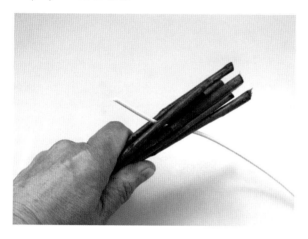

> **Note**
> To be able to more clearly see the progression of the knot, the photos show a piece of rattan.

2. Bring the stem out to the front and around the foot, which is sticking out from the middle of the bundle, and then bring it back under the bundle.

3. Bring the stem up to the front on the other side and again bring it around the base.

4. Continue the same progression, bringing it around the base and then under the bundle each time until a design starts to appear. On the back side the stem always stays parallel to itself.

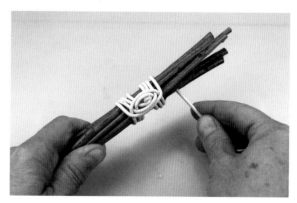

5. Finish the knot by securing the stem under the previous round.

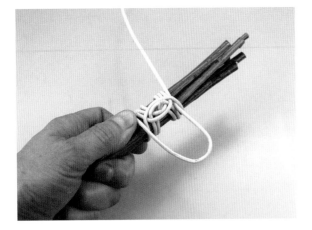

6. Pull on the stem to lock the knot. Cut it at ¼ in. (0.6 cm).

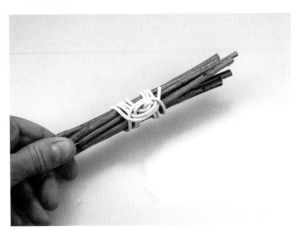

The Japanese knot appears in two projects in this book: the flower holder (below left) and the bird feeder (below right).

TIPS AND GLOSSARY

BASKET-MAKING BASICS

To make baskets that are evenly woven and well proportioned, there are certain basic rules that should be followed.

- Size of spokes: Always choose spokes that are larger in diameter to support the thinner weavers. If you do not have thick enough spokes, you can double them up.

- Relative position of the spokes and weavers: Weavers must pass back and forth between the spokes in such a way that the latter remain straight.

- Rigidity of a basket: Even spaces between each spoke will result in a basket that will remain solid and keep its shape—for example, for wicker, spaces between spokes should be around 1 in. (2.5 cm).

WORKING POSITION

You can work either at a table or on your knees, using a cloth to protect you from getting wet and dirty.

Your right hand is used to guide the weavers in front of and behind the spokes, gently pulling on them, while your left hand, with fingers spread open (like a comb), pushes down on the weave to prevent holes (reverse for left-handers).

STORAGE OF MATERIALS

Keep leaves and stems in a well-ventilated area away from the light. Store bark in a cardboard or wooden box.

GLOSSARY

Border: Final interweaving of spokes to produce a finished edge on a project.

Cordage: Type of rope made from strands of plant fibers.

Ligature: Way to tie together a bundle of fibers. The Japanese knot is a decorative ligature often used in basket weaving.

Spoke: Vertical element forming the rigid framework for weaving the sides of the basket.

Strand: Leaf or group of leaves wound together to form cordage.

Stroke: A weaving style or technique such as twining, triple twining, double randing, and so forth.

Twining: A weave using two weavers, in which the spokes partially show through.

Triple twining: A weave using three weavers, denser than regular twining. It strengthens the weaving at the base and keeps the spokes in place.

Weaving the sides: Filling the walls of a basket-weaving project.

Woven fibers basketry: Basket-making technique that comes closest to weaving. It most often uses soft fibers, which frequently involves the use of molds.

IRIS
LEAVES

CHILI PEPPER RISTRA

If you want to store your harvest of chili peppers, drying requires time. This project helps you do it in a decorative way and introduces you to making two-strand cordage.

MATERIALS

- 1 small handful of iris leaves
- 12 red chili peppers
- Basic kit (see p. 10)

Size of finished ristra: 16 in. (40 cm) long

INSTRUCTIONS

Two-Strand Cordage

1. Using iris leaves, make two pieces of cordage approximately ⅛ in. (3 mm) in diameter and 3 ft. (1 m) long (see "Techniques," p. 18); then make one small, thin cord approximately ¹⁄₁₆ in. (1.5 mm) in diameter and 1 ft. (30 cm) long.

2. Fold each piece of cordage into two equal parts.

3. Place one piece of cordage on top of the other. Using the thin cord, wrap them together about 1½ in. (4 cm) from the folded end and knot the small cord, forming a loop for hanging.

Weaving In the Chili Peppers

4. Lay the four lengths of cordage flat and place a pepper perpendicular to them, near the loop for hanging. Bring two of the cords over the pepper, so that you have the configuration shown below: two cords under the pepper and two cords over.

5. Place the two cords on the top between the two cords on the bottom. Lift up the cords from the bottom, lay a new pepper on the remaining two cords, lower the now-top cords on top of the pepper, and place them between the cords on the bottom.

6. Continue weaving in all the peppers. Braid below the last pepper, and then knot the end of the cords to complete the ristra.

DOUBLE HEART

A heart woven from iris leaves brings a romantic touch to your home, or use it to decorate your Christmas table with natural colors.

MATERIALS

- 1 handful of iris leaves
- A few small sticks, pinecones, and alder fruit
- Basic kit (see p. 10)
- Hot glue gun and glue stick

Size of finished double heart: 8¼ in. (21 cm) high and 6¼ in. (16 cm) wide

INSTRUCTIONS

Braiding

1. With the iris leaves, make four braids 16 in. (40 cm) long and ¾ in. (2 cm) wide and then two small braids 7 in. (18 cm) long and ⅜ in. (1 cm) wide.

Tying

2. With the linen twine, securely tie together the two small braids at the base of the braiding.

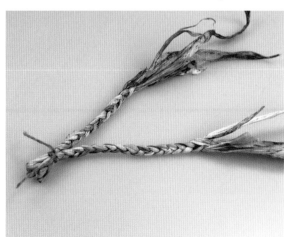

3. Tie a knot at the other end of the small braids to form the smaller heart.

4. Tie a knot at the base of the other four braids lying side by side.

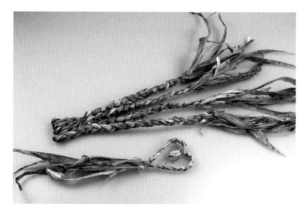

5. Form the large heart by folding down the braids, two on each side, joining them back together again at the point of the heart.

6. Place the point of the small heart inside that of the large heart. Tie all the ends of the braids together with twine.

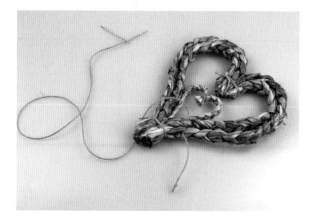

Finishing

7. Trim the ends of the large heart to a point. On each side, sew together the two braids that are next to each other.

8. Attach a loop of linen twine at the top of the heart for hanging.

9. Use the glue gun to attach the decorative items on the upper point of the heart—a small bunch of sticks, pinecones, and alder fruit.

CATTAIL
LEAVES

NESTING BASKETS

The practical thing about these baskets is that they can go anywhere you want—the kitchen, living room, and so on—and hold whatever you'd like. No more excuses for not putting things away!

INSTRUCTIONS FOR SMALL BASKET

Base

1. Select twelve thick cattail leaves and cut them so they measure 25 in. (65 cm) long.

2. Put the leaves one on top of the other in pairs, top to tail, and weave the base of your basket (see "Techniques," p. 21).

3. With a thinner leaf, start a twining weave around the base (see "Techniques," p. 26).

4. Still using thinner leaves, continue to twine until the base is 2¾ in. (7 cm) in diameter.

MATERIALS

- Cattail leaves
- Basic kit (see p. 10)
- Rigid containers (bottle, canning jar, tin can)

Size of finished baskets: Small one is 7 in. (18 cm) high by 2¾ in. (7 cm) in diameter; medium one is 4¼ in. (11 cm) high by 4¾ in. (12 cm) in diameter; large one is 2½ in. (6.5 cm) high by 6¾ in. (17 cm) in diameter

Weaving

5. Turn the base over and place a bottle in the center. Stand the leaves up against the bottle and continue to weave, alternating between twining and randing (see "Techniques," p. 21) until the basket is 7 in. (18 cm) high. Press the leaves against the container while you weave.

INSTRUCTIONS FOR MEDIUM BASKET

Base

1. Select twelve thick cattail leaves and cut them so they measure 20 in. (50 cm) long.

2. Make the base in the same way as for the small basket, twining until it measures 4¾ in. (12 cm) in diameter.

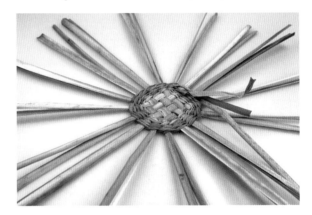

Border

6. Finish with the woven border (see "Techniques," p. 23). Cut the end of the leaves ⅜ in. (1 cm) from the weaving.

Weaving

3. Turn the base over and place a canning jar in the center. Stand the leaves up against the jar and twine the weavers until the basket is 4 in. (10 cm) high.

Border

4. Start the woven border (see "Techniques," p. 23).

5. Twine the weavers for three rounds to finish the border. Cut the end of the leaves ⅜ in. (1 cm) from the weaving.

INSTRUCTIONS FOR LARGE BASKET

Base

1. Select twenty-four thick cattail leaves and cut them so they measure 20 in. (50 cm) long.

2. Start the base in the same way as for the two other baskets, twining until it measures 6¾ in. (17 cm) in diameter.

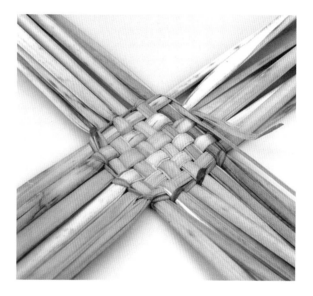

Weaving

3. Turn the base over and place a tin can in the center. Stand the leaves up against the can and continue to twine until the basket is 2⅜ in. (6 cm) high.

4. Weave the last round, separating all the leaves.

Border

5. Make the woven border (see "Techniques," p. 23).

6. Twine two rounds to finish the border. Cut the end of the leaves ⅜ in. (1 cm) from the weaving.

LETTER HOLDER

This natural letter holder will bring the outdoors into your entryway or office. The harmonious pairing of willow and cattail makes for a unique design.

MATERIALS

- 1 large handful of cattail leaves
- 1 willow stem, 4 ft. (1.2 m)
- Basic kit (see p. 10)

Size of finished letter holder: 10¼ in. (26 cm) high by 9 in. (23 cm) wide

INSTRUCTIONS

Structure

1. With an Opinel-style knife, make a notch 12 in. (30 cm) from the base of the willow stem.

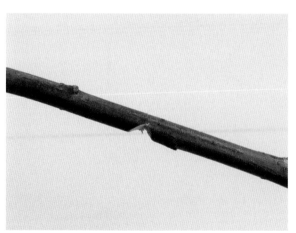

2. Fold the stem at the notch. Arch the rest of the stem and attach it with twine to hold the structure in the shape of a stirrup.

3. Select twenty-six thick cattail leaves and cut them to measure about 18 in. (45 cm) long.

4. Lay them one on top of the other in pairs and tie them to the base of the stirrup. To do this, fold each pair in half, place the ends around the base of the stirrup, and slide the free ends through the loop end. Pull to firmly tie the leaves to the base.

5. Repeat this process for the remaining twelve pairs.

Weaving

6. Start weaving by bringing a long leaf around the left side of the stirrup.

7. Separate the leaves in half, pushing them to each side of the stirrup and start circular twining (see "Techniques," p. 26).

8. Continue weaving until 4 in. (10 cm) high. To make the letter holder a little wider, temporarily place some plastic bags inside.

9. Weave the last round, separating all the leaves.

Border

10. Make the woven border (see "Techniques," p. 23).

11. Twine two rounds to finish the border.

12. Twine two additional rounds to shape a curve on the front side that, at the center, dips down 1 in. (2.5 cm) below the opening.

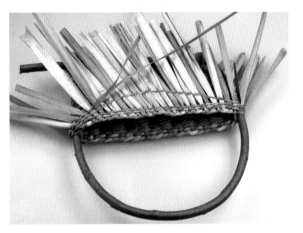

13. Cut the end of the leaves ³⁄₈ in. (1 cm) from the weaving.

SHOULDER BAG

Here is something to bring a touch of nature into your summer wardrobe. Some braided leaves and careful weaving, and this outstanding bag can come along on all your countryside outings.

MATERIALS

- 1 large handful of cattail leaves
- 1 willow stem, $2^3/_8$ in. (6 cm)
- Basic kit (see p. 10)
- Sewing thread matching the color of the leaves
- Adhesive tape
- Sewing machine
- Pins
- Rolling machine or rolling pin
- Drill and $^1/_8$ in. (3 mm) wood drill bit or gimlet
- Matchstick or small dowel

Size of finished bag: $7^1/_4$ in. (18 cm) high by 10 in. (25 cm) wide with a 37 in. (95 cm) long strap

INSTRUCTIONS

Braiding

1. Braid about 30 ft. (9 m) of four-strand braid for the bag and 5 ft. (1.5 m) for the strap (see "Techniques," p. 24).

2. Pass the entire length of the braid through the rolling machine or flatten with a rolling pin (this step makes the braid more pliable and limits shrinkage from drying).

Sewing

3. Fold the long braid $7^3/_4$ in. (20 cm) from the end. Flatten the fold well to facilitate machine stitching.

4. With the sewing machine, sew the braid edge to edge with a zigzag stitch, until three widths have been sewn together (bottom of the bag).

5. Pivot the bottom of the bag and continue stitching an uninterrupted seam. Take the time to carefully position the braid to stitch together the edges of the strip along the entire length.

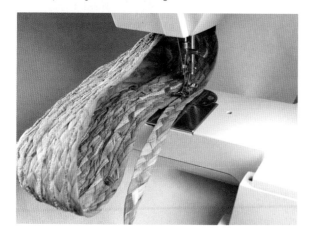

6. Sew until the bag is fifteen braids high. Stop sewing in the middle of the bag.

7. Leave an extra 7 in. (18 cm) of unattached braid at the end. Cut off any excess and wrap about 1¼ in. (3 cm) at the end with adhesive tape.

Closure

8. Make a loop with the end of the braid. Pin it to the inside of the bag to keep it in place and machine stitch.

Strap

9. Wrap the two ends of the braid made for the strap with adhesive tape. Again using a zigzag stitch, sew down the center of the length of the strap to strengthen it.

10. Position the ends of the strap inside the narrow sides. Sew them on firmly, going back and forth several times with a zigzag stitch.

Finishing

11. With the drill or the gimlet, make a hole through the middle of the willow stem, like a button.

12. Position the wicker button on the front of the bag, perpendicular to the braids, using the closure loop to help determine its placement. Place a matchstick or small dowel between the button and the bag; then sew the button onto the bag with linen twine (the space created by the matchstick will give the button some mobility and make it easier to place the loop around it). Remove the matchstick.

STOOL COVER

You can give a folding stool new life by replacing the seat cover with a handwoven fiber mat. This method of weaving may also be used to make placemats or table runners.

MATERIALS

- 1 large handful of cattail leaves (approximately fifty-four leaves of the same width)
- 1 folding stool with a screwed-on seat about 8 in. (20 cm) in diameter
- Basic kit (see p. 10)
- Sewing machine
- Staple gun
- Rolling pin

Size of finished seat cover: 12 in. (30 cm) in diameter

INSTRUCTIONS

Weaving

1. Cut the cattail leaves so they measure 16 in. (40 cm) long.

2. Select eight leaves and place them flat and horizontal on your work surface. Holding them down with your left hand, start vertical weaving with a new leaf. Follow these steps: Starting from the top, take the new leaf under two leaves and then over two leaves, and so on.

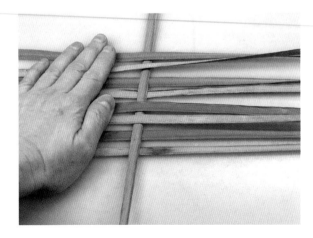

3. Weave in a second leaf, taking it first under one leaf and then over two leaves; then continue with the previous pattern. Doing so shifts the pattern by one leaf in comparison with the first leaf woven in.

4. Weave in the third leaf, bringing it over two leaves and then under two leaves, and so on.

5. Weave in a fourth leaf, bringing it over one leaf and then under two leaves, alternating every two leaves.

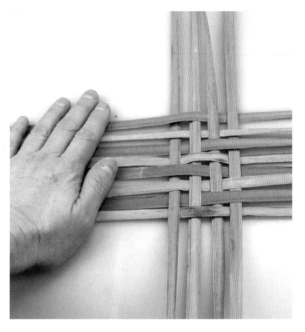

6. Continue weaving in the same pattern as for the first four leaves.

7. Continue to weave following the same pattern, adding leaves horizontally and vertically.

8. Weave a square approximately 12½ in. by 12½ in. (32 by 32 cm) that will cover the stool seat.

9. Stitch a zigzag stitch by machine around the perimeter to stabilize the edge of the weaving.

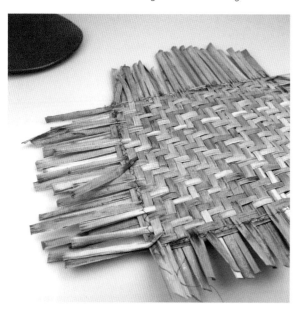

10. Flatten the mat with the rolling pin to limit shrinkage when drying.

Assembly

11. Unscrew the seat and place it right-side-down on the wrong side of the mat. Fold down the edges of the mat and staple to the seat starting on opposite sides.

12. Continue to staple fairly close together around the perimeter of the seat, being careful not to obstruct the placement of the screws. Cut off extra mat with scissors.

Finishing

13. Let dry for 24 hours; then place the seat back on the stool and screw it on.

VASE

My preference is for useful, simple, and stripped-down items, like this vase that has a coastal, nautical vibe.

MATERIALS

- 12 cattail leaves
- 1 ornamental plum or willow stem
- Basic kit (see p. 10)
- Glass jar (like an asparagus jar)
- Cork stopper attached to 1 large needle (see step 1)

Size of finished vase: 8 in. (20 cm) high and 3½ in. (9 cm) in diameter

INSTRUCTIONS

Preparation of Leaves

1. To make the thin cordage that will be used for the net, split the cattail leaves lengthwise in half and then into fourths using a needle attached to a cork.

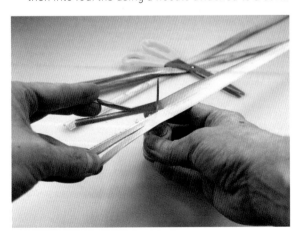

Rope Net

2. Using these narrow strips of leaf, make 8 ft. (2.5 m) of thin double-strand cordage that is about ¹⁄₁₆–¹⁄₈ in. (1.5–3 mm) thick, depending on the original width of the leaves (see "Techniques," p. 18).

3. Cut off any ends that stick out. Open up the loop at the base of the cordage and slide the other end through it to form a lasso that is the diameter of the jar.

4. Create looped stitches around the lasso, intertwining them. To do this, bring the end of the cordage under the lasso and then through the little loop just created (for embroiderers, this technique resembles the blanket stitch or buttonhole stitch).

5. Set up a ring of thirteen stitches all the way around the starting lasso.

6. Continue weaving the net in this way for two more rounds. Place the jar inside to check that the starting diameter has not changed.

7. Continue making another 21 ft. (6.5 m) or so of cordage; then continue weaving the net, removing the jar.

Finishing

8. When the net is the height of the jar, place the jar back inside. Without cutting the cordage, tie a knot in the first loop of the round.

9. Cut four pieces of an ornamental plum stem and attach them to the knot with the cordage.

HAT

You're going to love this cattail hat with its charming brim! Made using a custom mold, it will be a constant companion in the summer.

INSTRUCTIONS

Hat Mold

1. With the wire, make a circle the size of your head.

2. On the sheet of polystyrene, trace the perimeter of this circle two times. Using a utility knife, cut out two identical forms and then glue one on top of the other.

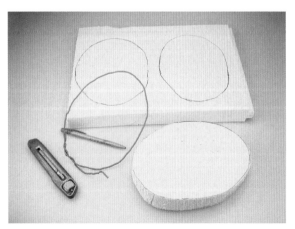

3. Round out the edges of this hat mold with sandpaper.

MATERIALS

- 1 large handful of cattail leaves
- Basic kit (see p. 10)
- Upholstery nails
- Small glass jar (like a little yogurt jar)

For the mold

- Sheet of extruded polystyrene, 1¾ in. (4.5 cm) thick
- 27½ in. (70 cm) of electrical wire or regular wire
- Special glue for polystyrene
- Medium sandpaper

Size of finished hat (custom-made hat size will vary): For a head size of 22 in. (56 cm): 3½ in. (9 cm) high, 13¾ in. (35 cm) wide, and 14½ in. (37 cm) long

Base

4. Select thick cattail leaves and cut them to the following sizes:

- 20 leaves 27½ in. (70 cm) long
- 12 leaves 25 in. (65 cm) long
- 2 leaves 14 in. (35 cm) long

5. Place the 27½ in. (70 cm) leaves and the 25 in. (65 cm) leaves on top of each other in pairs, top to tail; then weave the base of the hat over/under until you have a 5½ in. by 3½ in. (14 by 9 cm) rectangle (see "Techniques," p. 21). The 27½ in. (70 cm) leaves are used for the length and the 25 in. (65 cm) ones for the width.

6. Weave the pair of 14 in. (35 cm) leaves along the width of the base. Adding this last pair is necessary for continuous over/under weaving with an uneven amount of spokes.

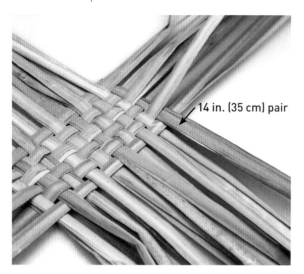

14 in. (35 cm) pair

7. Place the woven base on the mold, right side facing you, and hold in place with an upholstery nail in each corner.

8. Select a narrow leaf and start on the side of the short 14 in. (35 cm) pair with over/under weaving.

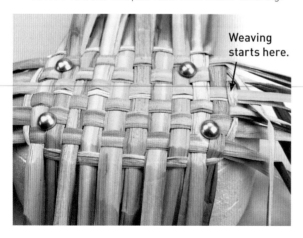

Weaving starts here.

9. Continue weaving for the height of the mold, being sure to press it flat against the sides. New leaves are added by overlapping the start and end of the leaves for about 1¾ in. (4.5 cm).

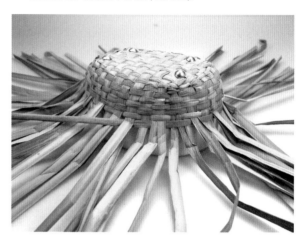

Brim

10. Once it is the right height, lay the leaves out flat on your work surface or on a table.

11. Twine a round with a long, thin leaf. This woven round makes it possible to flatten the structure of the hat against the mold and prepares for weaving the brim.

12. Weave the base of the hat brim, continuing to weave flat for 1½ in. (4 cm).

13. Divide each spoke into two in order to weave around each leaf. This way the spaces between the spokes will not be too wide and will provide better support for the weaving. To keep an uneven number of spokes, add one leaf. Insert it wherever you'd like in the weave. Continue weaving for another 1½ in. (4 cm).

Border

14. Split a long leaf in half, narrower than the spokes, and then twine a round (see "Techniques," p. 26). This round will lock in the 3 in. (8 cm) of weaving.

15. One by one, roll the end of each spoke and place it behind the following spoke. The ends are now on top of the brim.

16. To make it easier to continue weaving the border, cut the spokes 2 in. (5 cm) from the edge and split them in half lengthwise with scissors.

17. Split a long, thin leaf in half and use it to twine two rounds.

Finishing

18. Roll a small glass jar around the border of the hat to flatten it and help prevent too much shrinkage when drying.

19. Cut all the spokes ⅜ in. (1 cm) from the weaving around the border.

SLIPPERS

Making your own slippers takes patience, but what satisfaction when you can finally slide your feet inside! It would be a shame to miss out on it. Follow these instructions word for word, and all will go well.

MATERIALS

- 1 large handful of cattail leaves per slipper
- Willow sticks
- Basic kit (see p. 10)

For the sole

- Piece of cardboard
- Felt tip pen

Size of finished slippers (custom-made slippers will vary in size): For women's size 6½ as shown: 3 in. (8 cm) high, 4¼ in. (11 cm) wide, and 10 in. (25 cm) long

INSTRUCTIONS

Pattern for the Sole

1. On a piece of cardboard, use the felt tip pen to draw around one of your feet or shoes. Cut out the pattern traced.

2. Measure the narrowest part of the heel (here 2¾ in. [7 cm]), divide this number in half, and mark this measurement around the interior perimeter of the sole, as shown in the photo. Draw the center of the slipper by following the marks (shown in yellow).

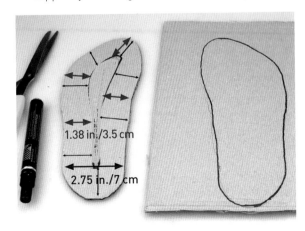

1.38 in./3.5 cm

2.75 in./7 cm

Sole

3. With six medium leaves folded in half, make a three-strand braid measuring 13 ft. (4 m) long (see "Techniques," p. 20). The braid should measure approximately ⅝ in. (1.5 cm) wide and 5/16 in. (8 mm) thick. Use a spray bottle to keep the braid moist the whole time you are making the slippers.

4. Fold the end of the braid over 3½ in. (9 cm) (on its smallest side). Sew in place with the needle and linen twine.

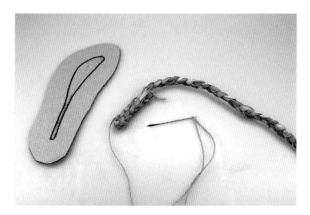

5. Place this folded end on the pattern and fill in the center of the sole with more of the braid. Take the time to perfectly adjust the length to ensure that the slippers won't be too small.

6. Sew the center of the sole, pulling your stitching tight, as the braid will expand slightly when drying.

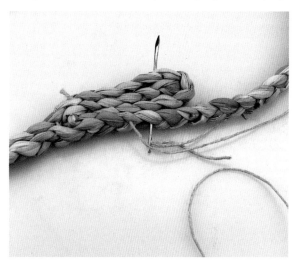

7. Sew the remainder of the braid until the pattern is completely filled in.

Sides

8. Gradually sew the braid onto the side of the sole, starting at a slight angle.

9. Continue to sew the braid around for four rounds (until reaching the desired height of the heel), using invisible stitching so the linen twine is hidden as much as possible. For sizes larger than 6½, you may need to add another round and thus extend the length of the braid.

Top

10. Try on your slipper and make a pattern from cardboard to cover the forefoot.

11. With three medium leaves folded in half, make a three-strand braid 29½ in. (75 cm) long. The braid must measure approximately ⅜ in. (1 cm) wide and 3/16 in. (0.5 cm) thick.

12. With the linen twine, sew the front upper like a snail in the shape and size of your pattern.

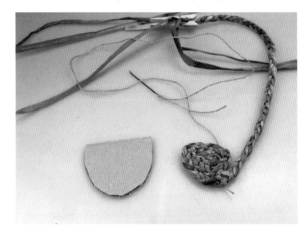

13. When the shape has been created, thin out the braid by cutting out one leaf from each strand and inserting all the ends into the braid using the needle.

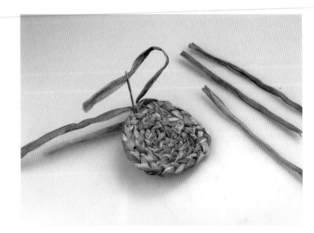

14. Sew the front upper to the top of the slipper with a leaf split in half. Before starting to sew, test the strength of the leaf by pulling on it. You can continue sewing with the linen twine if desired.

Finishing

15. Thin out the braid that was used to make the sides of the slipper by cutting out leaves from each strand. Then insert the end of the strands into the braid with the needle and trim any ends sticking out.

16. Cut three pieces of wicker in decreasing sizes. With a needle and the twine, attach them to the top of the slipper.

Second Slipper

17. Make the second slipper in the same way, starting with the same pattern. Simply turn the sole over when you are ready to sew the sides (step 8), to avoid making another slipper for the same foot.

WILLOW
STEMS

SPANISH PLATTER

Used as a cheese platter, fruit basket, or valet tray, this decorative platter will find a special place on your dining table or in your kitchen. This atypical weaving resembles the bottom of Spanish baskets.

MATERIALS

Structure

- 2 willow stems, 5 ft. (1.5 m)

Weaving of the platter

- 20 or so willow stems, 4 ft. (1.2 m)
- 8 ornamental plum stems, about 20–24 in. (50–60 cm) (depending on gardener's pruning)

Weaving of points

- 4 willow stems, 32 in. (80 cm)

- Basic kit (see p. 10)
- Large tin can or pail

Size of finished platter: 9 in. (23 cm) wide and 14 in. (35 cm) long

INSTRUCTIONS

Structure

1. While taking into account their natural curvature, make the two 5 ft. (1.5 m) stems more pliable by bending them around a large tin can or a pail.

2. Make a ring 8½ in. (22 cm) in diameter with the first stem; then twist the second stem around the first so their feet end up on opposite sides.

Weaving

3. Attach and stretch a piece of twine over the diameter of the ring. This string decreases the risk of the ring becoming misshapen while weaving the platter.

4. With the 4 ft. (1.2 m) stems, cut four spokes 17¾ in. (45 cm) long and place them tip to toe in pairs. Divide the spokes on both sides of the center of the ring.

5. Start weaving in the center and parallel to the string. On the left side of the ring, place a 4 ft. (1.2 m) stem under the ring, and then weave over/under and over the ring. Weave the second stem in the same manner, starting on the right side of the ring. Then move the two stems together.

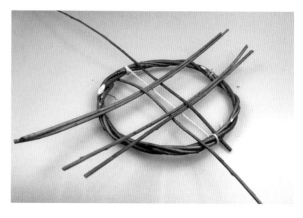

6. Insert the foot of a new stem on the left under the ring and hold it with your left hand. With your right hand, lift the stem and place it above the first two spokes, then under the following two spokes, and finally over the ring. The platter can be quickly and easily woven following this technique.

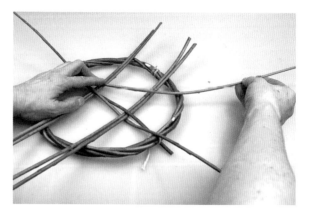

7. Weave twelve willow stems in this way, followed by the eight ornamental plum stems on either side.

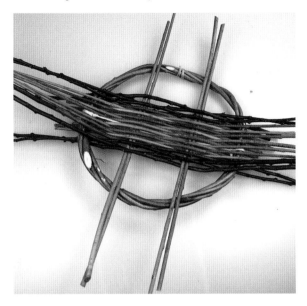

8. Continue weaving. Don't hesitate to cut the stems 1¼ in. (3 cm) from the outside edge of the ring to reuse them for weaving.

Weaving the Points

9. Insert the base of one of the four 32 in. (80 cm) stems under the ring and weave in a figure 8 pattern around the two spokes. Continue weaving with a second stem, always starting with the foot.

10. Move the pair of spokes together to create a point. Finish the weaving in a figure 8 up to the point; it will simply be locked in by the weaving.

11. Complete the other point in the same manner.

Finishing

12. Evenly cut off all the ends of the stems. Place the pruning shears against the ring to follow its curve.

13. Cut the points ⅝ in. (1.5 cm) from the weaving.

BIRD FEEDER

Peacefully watching the birds through the window: a perfect reason to make a wicker bird feeder.

MATERIALS

- 12 willow stems, 4 ft. (1.2 m)
- 6 willow stems, 39 in. (100 cm)
- 8 willow stems, 32 in. (80 cm)
- Basic kit (see p. 10)
- Wood base, about 8 in. by 8 in. (20 by 20 cm) and 4¾ in. (12 cm) high
- Drill and 5/16 in. (8 mm) diameter wood drill bit

Size of finished feeder: 17 in. (43 cm) long and 4¾ in. (12 cm) in diameter; handle 4¾ in. (12 cm) high

INSTRUCTIONS

1. Using the drill and the drill bit, drill twelve 5/16 in. (8 mm) holes in the wood base so that they form a circle 4¾ in. (12 cm) in diameter.

2. Place the feet of the twelve 4 ft. (1.2 m) stems in the holes. Fold a 39 in. (100 cm) stem in half and place it around one of the spokes.

3. Start by twining (see "Techniques," p. 26). Twine the stems for four rounds.

4. Attach the tips of the spokes together with twine to hold them in place.

5. Weave in a figure 8 pattern around two spokes with a 32 in. (80 cm) stem, beginning with its foot.

6. Continue with a second stem, this time beginning with the tip.

7. Weave three other columns in the same way.

8. Take the feeder off the wood base. Cut off the twelve spokes ¾ in. (2 cm) from the base of the weaving and at about 18 in. (45 cm) high.

9. Hold the twelve spokes together with a Japanese knot made with one of the 39 in. (100 cm) stems (see "Techniques," p. 31).

Handle

10. Insert the foot of a 39 in. (100 cm) stem into the twining. Curve the stem and place it from the inside to the outside of the feeder under two rounds of weaving.

11. Twist the stem around itself. Finish the handle and lock the tip into the weave. Trim off any excess.

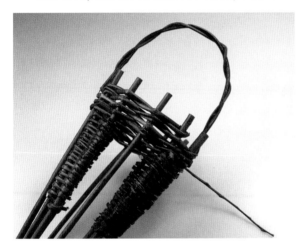

FLOWER HOLDERS

To get your children started with gardening, you can suggest they stick pots into these flower holders and transplant their favorite flowers in them. And if you'd rather use these holders for candles, that will work, too.

MATERIALS (MAKES 3)

- 33 thin willow stems, 4 ft. (1.2 m)
- 3 willow stems, 32 in. (80 cm)
- 3 large sweet chestnut or hazel stems (sticks), 25 in. (65 cm)
- Basic kit (see p. 10)

Size of finished flower holder: 28 in. (72 cm) high, bowl is 4 in. (10 cm) in diameter and 3 in. (8 cm) high

> **Note**
> It is very important to select thin stems, as the spiral weave starts out with the foot (and not the tip) of the stems.

INSTRUCTIONS

There are more stems than what is used for the spiral stitch explained in the "Techniques" section, but the principle stays the same.

1. Place the feet of eleven wicker stems around the base of one of the sweet chestnut or hazel sticks. Keep them in place with a zip tie and distribute the feet of the stems evenly around the circumference of the stick.

2. Place a second zip tie ¾ in. (2 cm) from the first one. Pull it tight to lock everything in place.

3. Using the pruning knife, one by one bend down the wicker stems even with the end of the stick.

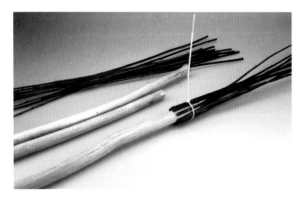

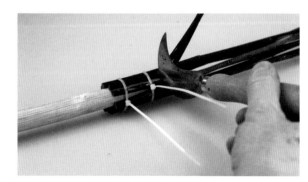

4. Spread open the bunch of stems and start the spiral weaving (see "Techniques," p. 29). Spray the wicker stems often to keep them pliable.

5. Weave to the end of the stems. The bowl shape will appear little by little.

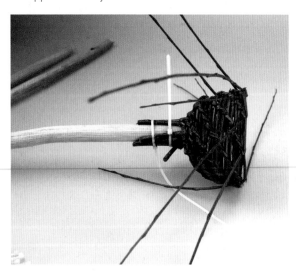

6. Insert the tip of the last stem under another one to secure it.

Finishing

7. Make a Japanese knot using a 32 in. (80 cm) wicker stem between the two zip ties for a beautiful finish (see "Techniques," p. 31).

8. Cut off the two ties.

9. Make the other two flower holders in the same way.

WALL SCONCE

Easy to make, this sconce will elegantly bring nature right into your home. It features different-colored branches and produces a warm, soft light.

MATERIALS

- 20 willow stems, 13 in. (33 cm)
- 20 ornamental plum stems, 13 in. (33 cm)
- 4 strips of sweet chestnut bark, 13 in. (33 cm) long
- Basic kit (see p. 10)
- Half-cylinder wall sconce frame, 10 in. (25 cm) high and 10 in. (25 cm) wide

Size of finished sconce: 14 in. (35 cm) high and 8½ in. (22 cm) wide

INSTRUCTIONS

1. Cut a strip of bark 13 in. (33 cm) long and ³/₁₆ in. (0.5 cm) wide. Position it on the rounded bottom edge of the frame. Tie it on firmly in the left corner with linen twine.

2. Lay the first stem vertically on the frame and attach it to the frame with a cross stitch. It must be 3 in. (8 cm) longer overall.

3. Place the second and then the third stem next to the first and attach them in the same way.

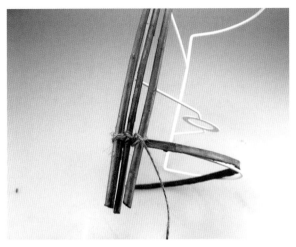

4. To personalize your sconce, play with the colors and placement of the stems, not necessarily all aligned.

5. Attach the stems to the top of the frame in the same manner.

6. Cut ten narrow strips of bark ³⁄₁₆ in. (0.5 cm) wide.

7. Weave the narrow strips over/under the stems, using your creativity to spread them out and create a design. Weave four narrow strips in front of where the lightbulb will be to reduce and soften the light.

BASKET

What would a basket-weaving book be without a basket pattern? If you want to bring a snack along on an outdoor adventure, this little atypically shaped basket will be your ideal companion. Bon appétit!

MATERIALS

- 20 willow stems, 4 ft. (1.2 m) (18 for the structure and 2 for reinforcing the handle)
- 53 willow stems, 39 in. (100 cm) (10 for twining the base, 18 for triple twining, and 25 for double randing)
- 4 willow stems, 32 in. (80 cm)
- 1 handful of iris leaves
- Basic kit (see p. 10)
- Round slice of wood, 3 in. (8 cm) in diameter and ⅝ in. (1.5 cm) thick
- Drill and ¼–⁵⁄₁₆ in. (6–8 mm) wood drill bit

Size of finished basket: 7¾ in. (20 cm) in diameter and 8¼ in. (21 cm) high; handle 16½ in. (42 cm) long

INSTRUCTIONS

Base

1. Drill fourteen holes ³⁄₁₆ in. (0.5 cm) in diameter, spaced about ⅝ in. (1.5 cm) apart, into the thickness of the round piece of wood.

2. Trim to a point the foot of fourteen of the 4 ft. (1.2 m) stems and insert them into the drilled holes.

3. With the 39 in. (100 cm) stems, twine three rounds around the spokes (see "Techniques," p. 26). Insert four new 4 ft. (1.2 m) willow stems into the weave, spacing them out evenly, and continue weaving until the base measures 7½ in. (19 cm) in diameter.

4. With the pruning knife, stand the spokes upright at the base of the weaving.

Weaving the Sides

5. Weave three rounds in triple twining with the 39 in. (100 cm) stems (see "Techniques," p. 27).

6. Still using the 39 in. (100 cm) stems, begin a double randing weave, starting with the foot of the stems,

until it measures 3 in. (8 cm) high (see "Techniques," p. 27).

7. Weave two additional rounds in triple twining.

8. Using the iris leaves, make an 8 ft. (2.4 m) long three-strand braid (see "Techniques," p. 20).

9. Insert the end of the braid down by one of the spokes; then start weaving in an over one/under one spoke sequence.

10. Because of the even number of spokes (eighteen), the weaving will not automatically alternate on each round. To keep weaving in the same pattern, start the second round by bringing the weaver in front of two spokes, and then return to the under one/over one spoke sequence. Continue in this manner until the entire braid has been woven in.

11. Tie the end of the braid with a piece of twine. Place the end inside the basket and cut off the excess.

12. Still using the 39 in. (100 cm) stems, weave two more rounds in triple twining.

Border

13. Bend a spoke using the awl and weave the border in the over one/under one spoke sequence for the next eight spokes, which is half the circumference of the basket.

14. Change direction by turning around the last spoke and weaving back in the opposite direction, still following the same sequence. To finish, the tip of the stem rests inside the basket, against the second spoke.

15. Bend the second spoke and proceed as for the first one, weaving in the same over/under sequence around the next seven spokes.

16. Continue weaving over the next five spokes in the same manner, taking the weaver completely around the last spoke every other time.

17. Follow this same pattern to weave the second half of the border, so that each half of the border forms shallow steps over nine spokes. Use the awl to precisely bend the spokes.

Handle

18. Insert a 4 ft. (1.2 m) stem alongside each spoke of the handle. Weave a 32 in. (80 cm) stem in a figure 8 pattern at the base on one side of the handle. Do the same for the other side.

19. Soak the stems that form the handle in water for 5 minutes to keep them pliable for twisting the handle.

20. Twist the entire length of the three stems on one side of the handle; then insert them from the outside to the inside of the basket under the figure 8 weave.

21. Twist the other side in the same manner. Finally, twist the two parts together.

22. With one of the thinner stems, encircle the base of the handle to secure and hide the end.

Finishing

23. Trim off all the ends of the stems at an angle.

24. Let the basket dry for about 24 hours in a well-ventilated area out of direct sunlight.

BARK

WINDMILL EARRINGS

These earrings, as well as the next ones, are made from tree bark and are ideal to give as an original gift. They will give you the perfect opportunity to practice the "windmill" knot.

MATERIALS

- 2 strips of mimosa bark, 8 in. (20 cm) long and ³/₈ in. (1 cm) wide
- 4 strips of mimosa bark, 6 in. (15 cm) long and ³/₈ in. (1 cm) wide
- 6 rocaille beads
- Two ⁵/₈ in. (1.5 cm) fishhook ear wires
- Thin metal wire
- Basic kit (see p. 10)
- Round nose jewelry pliers

Size of finished earrings: 2 in. (5 cm) long and 1 in. (2.5 cm) wide

> **Note**
>
> The two pairs of earrings shown in this book are made of mimosa, whose bark has highly contrasting colors on the two sides, but you can easily use another thin bark, such as willow, forsythia, and so forth.

INSTRUCTIONS

1. Place an 8 in. (20 cm) strip around the index and middle finger of your left hand, bark facing you, and hold it in place with your thumb (right hand for left-handers).

2. Place a 6 in. (15 cm) strip perpendicular, in front of and then behind the first strip, with the inside of the bark facing you. About two-thirds of the strip will stick out on the left.

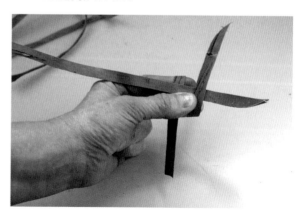

3. With the other hand, take the left end of the second strip and bring it around the front as shown in the photo. Place it in front of and then behind the strip that is going around your fingers.

4. Tighten the strip to make the knot. Pull the ends of the four strips in opposite directions to strengthen the knot.

5. Make a second knot on the first strip with the second 6 in. (15 cm) strip. Make sure the two knots are touching.

Assembly

6. Let dry for 12 hours while being pressed. Cut the excess off the strips at the end of the knots.

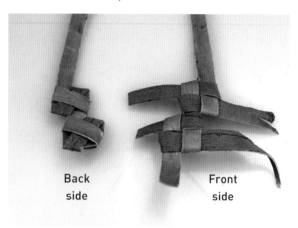

Back side   Front side

7. Wedge and bend the metal wire into the knot; then insert the first bead so that it is positioned at the center of the knot. Put the wire back in the knot and insert the second bead in the same manner. Add the third bead, make a loop to attach the ear wire, and secure the wire by twisting it around itself and hiding the twist in the earring.

8. With the round nose pliers, attach the ear wire to the earring.

9. Repeat the directions to make the second earring.

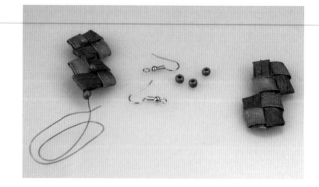

BOX KNOT EARRINGS

Here we showcase the natural beauty of bark while creating a unique final touch to an outfit.

MATERIALS

- 4 strips of mimosa bark, 16 in. (40 cm) long and $3/16$ in. (0.5 cm) wide
- 8 rocaille beads
- Two $5/8$ in. (1.5 cm) ear wires
- 2 flat-head pins, $1\frac{1}{2}$ in. (4 cm) long
- Basic kit (see p. 10)
- Round nose jewelry pliers

Size of finished earrings: $5/8$ in. (1.5 cm) high and $\frac{1}{2}$ in. (1.3 cm) diagonal

INSTRUCTIONS

1. As for the previous earrings, make a windmill knot with the two 16 in. (40 cm) strips, with one strip bark side up and the other back side up. Adjust to position the knot in the center of the strips.

2. Place the knot with the back side facing you. Fold down three consecutive strips clockwise, each going on top of the other.

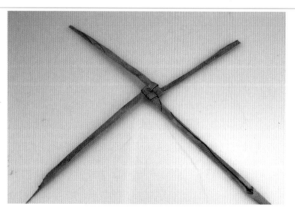

3. Bring the fourth strip over the third and under the first.

4. Continue in the same manner for the entire length of the bark strips. The weaving will measure ⅝ in. (1.5 cm) high.

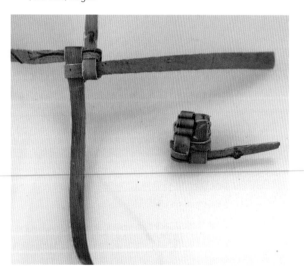

Assembly

5. Thread a bead onto the flat-head pin, and then pass the pin through the weaving and thread three more beads on top. Create a loop at the end of the pin with the round nose pliers and attach the ear wire.

6. Repeat the directions to make the second earring.

PENCIL HOLDER

Everyone always needs a little container to hold supplies. Here it is, in lovely natural colors.

MATERIALS

- 9 strips of sweet chestnut bark, 17¾ in. (45 cm) long and ½ in. (1.3 cm) wide
- 5 strips of sweet chestnut bark, 14 in. (35 cm) long and ½ in. (1.3 cm) wide
- About 15 long iris leaves
- Basic kit (see p. 10)
- Small board
- Upholstery nail
- Pencil
- Container, about 3¼ in. (8.5 cm) in diameter

Size of finished pencil holder: 4¼ in. (11 cm) high and 3½ in. (9 cm) in diameter

INSTRUCTIONS

Base

1. Make the star base (see "Techniques," p. 28). On the wrong side, use a pencil to mark the middle of the nine 17¾ in. (45 cm) strips. Place them one on top of the other and nail them in the middle to the board, wrong side facing up.

2. Fan them out evenly until a circle is formed. Use a pencil to mark on each strip the circumference of a circle measuring 3¼ in. (8.5 cm) in diameter.

3. Twine two rounds around the circumference of the circle with a piece of twine 51 in. (1.3 m) long (see "Techniques," p. 26), and tie a knot in it to finish the weaving (see "Techniques," p. 23).

Weaving the Sides

4. Stand up the spokes vertically and twine three rounds with the iris leaves.

5. Secure a 14 in. (35 cm) strip of bark behind a stake using a clothespin; then weave over a spoke/under a spoke all the way around.

6. Overlap the end of the strip with the beginning by 1¼ in. (3 cm), behind the stake. Cut off excess with scissors.

7. Twine four rounds with the iris leaves. To make it easier to weave while keeping the sides as straight as possible, place the container inside the holder.

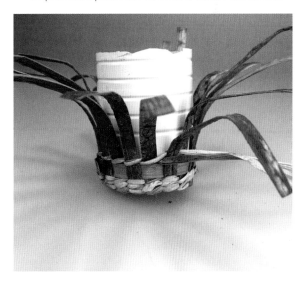

8. Weave three rows with the 14 in. (35 cm) strips of bark, playing with the different looks of the front and back sides.

9. Twine another three rounds with the iris leaves. Use the folding tool to even up the twining.

Handle

10. Make a sewn border. Remove the container and place a ½ in. (1.3 cm) wide strip of bark inside the holder, even with the edge of the weaving. Bend each spoke horizontally, one after the other. Attach them with the linen twine (see "Techniques," p. 28).

WALL BASKET

So romantic, this little wall basket can find a place in your entryway as well as in your bedroom. Add dried flowers for a decorative touch.

MATERIALS

Structure

- 5 strips of sweet chestnut bark, 21½ in. (55 cm) long and ⅝ in. (1.5 cm) wide
- 3 strips of sweet chestnut bark, 21½ in. (55 cm) long and ¾ in. (2 cm) wide

Sides

- 12 strips of sweet chestnut bark, 14 in. (35 cm) long and ⅝–¾ in. (1.5–2 cm) wide (depending on your bark)

Border

- 2 strips of sweet chestnut bark, 27½ in. (70 cm) long and ³⁄₁₆ in. (0.5 cm) wide

Hanger

- 1 strip of sweet chestnut bark, 8 in. (20 cm) long and ⁵⁄₁₆ in. (0.8 cm) wide

- Basic kit (see p. 10)
- Newspaper

Size of finished basket: 7 in. (18 cm) high and 4¾ in. (12 cm) wide

INSTRUCTIONS

Base

1. Place six of the 21½ in. (55 cm) long strips flat on your work surface, wrong side facing up (four strips of ⅝ in. (1.5 cm) wide and two strips of ¾ in. (2 cm) wide). Weave over/under with the remaining two 21½ in. strips (one ¾ in. wide and one ⅝ in. wide).

2. Be sure to line up the strips so that the weaving is centered.

3. Take a length of linen twine equal to two times the perimeter of the base plus 6 in. (15 cm) and fold it in half. Use it to twine one round to secure the weaving (see "Techniques," p. 26), and then tie a knot.

Weaving the Sides

4. Stand up the stakes of the basket using the folding tool.

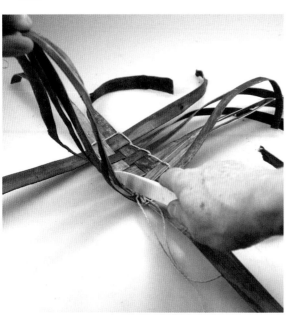

5. Secure a 14 in. (35 cm) strip of bark behind a stake on one of the narrow sides using a clothespin; then weave over a stake/under a stake all the way around the basket.

6. Overlap the end of the strip with the beginning by 1¼ in. (3 cm), behind the stake. Cut off excess strip with scissors.

7. Start weaving the strips on the narrow sides, alternating the side each round.

8. Weave the eleven remaining strips, forming the basket sides in the same way.

Border

9. Starting on one of the narrow sides, twine two rounds with the narrow strips of bark. This step can be fiddly, so allow yourself the time to do it well.

10. Dip the stakes and the top of the basket in warm water for a few seconds.

11. Trim the ends of the stakes to form a point. Fold them horizontally toward the inside and, using the folding tool, insert them into the twining.

Hanger

12. Secure the ends of the strip in the twining, leaving one strip width in between, and straighten it to use as a hanger.

Finishing

13. Stuff the inside of the wall basket with crunched-up newspaper. Let dry for 24 hours in a well-ventilated area away from the light.

TISSUE BOX COVER

The outside of a tissue box is rarely pretty, but you can remedy that problem with a woven bark box that you can place anywhere in the home and replace the inside box when empty.

MATERIALS

Structure

- 5 strips of sweet chestnut bark, 20 in. (50 cm) long and ¾ in. (2 cm) wide
- 10 strips of sweet chestnut bark, 16 in. (40 cm) long and ¾ in. (2 cm) wide

Sides

- 1 strip of sweet chestnut bark, 29½ in. (75 cm) long and ¾ in. (2 cm) wide
- 2 strips of sweet chestnut bark, 29½ in. (75 cm) long and ⅜ in. (1 cm) wide

Border

- 1 strip of sweet chestnut bark, 29½ in. (75 cm) long and ¾ in. (2 cm) wide

Opening

- 2 strips of sweet chestnut bark, 7½ in. (19 cm) long and ¾ in. (2 cm) wide
- 2 strips of sweet chestnut bark, 2⅜ in. (6 cm) long and ¾ in. (2 cm) wide

- 10 cattail leaves
- Basic kit (see p. 10)
- Rectangular tissue box

Size of finished box: 2⅜ in. (6 cm) high, 4¾ in. (12 cm) wide, and 10 in. (25 cm) long

INSTRUCTIONS

Base

1. Place two of the 20 in. (50 cm) long strips horizontally, flat on your work surface. Weave over/under vertically with two of the 16 in. (40 cm) strips. The woven part will be the upper-left corner on the top of the tissue box.

2. Continue to weave eight more vertical strips and three horizontal strips. Leave a ³⁄₁₆ in. (0.5 cm) space between strips for the following part of weaving the box.

3. Take a length of linen twine equal to two times the perimeter of the base plus 6 in. (15 cm) and fold it in half. Starting at the upper left corner, use it to twine one round to secure the weaving (see "Techniques," p. 26), and then tie a knot.

Weaving the Sides

4. Stand up the stakes using the folding tool.

5. Place the tissue box on the weaving, and then start twining with a cattail leaf split in half, again starting at the upper left corner. Twine two rounds.

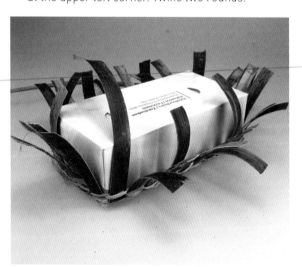

6. Weave three strips of the 29½ in. (75 cm) bark, with the ¾ in. (2 cm) strip between the two ⅜ in. (1 cm) strips. Start weaving on one of the narrow sides, changing sides with each weaver.

7. Weave three additional rounds with the cattail leaves.

Border

8. Remove the tissue box to start the woven border. Place the strip of ¾ in. (2 cm) bark on the inside.

9. One by one, bend each vertical strip horizontally toward the inside, and then attach them by sewing with a cattail leaf split in two (see "Techniques," p. 23). From time to time, insert the tissue box to ensure that it still fits.

Opening

10. Turn the box over, top side up. Cut the center horizontal strip, as well as the six center vertical strips, to create the opening.

11. Over this opening place the two 7½ in. (19 cm) strips horizontally and the two 2⅜ in. (6 cm) strips vertically. Hold them all in place with clothespins.

12. Sew on the strips with a cattail leaf split in two.

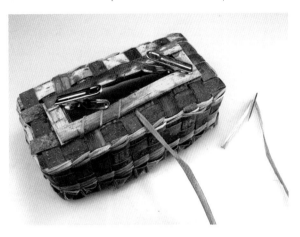

OPEN WEAVE BASKET

This basket is made with a typical Asian technique—triaxial weaving—that is used to create light, yet solid, items with few materials.

MATERIALS

Structure

- 12 strips of sweet chestnut bark, 27½ in. (70 cm) long and ¾ in. (2 cm) wide

Sides

- 3 strips of sweet chestnut bark, 35½ in. (90 cm) long and ¾ in. (2 cm) wide

Border

- 2 strips of sweet chestnut bark, 35½ in. (90 cm) long and ¾ in. (2 cm) wide

Decoration

- 24 strips of sweet chestnut bark, 10 in. (25 cm) long and ³⁄₁₆ in. (0.5 cm) wide

- Basic kit (see p. 10)
- 2 heavy rulers

Size of finished basket: 6¾ in. (17 cm) high and 10 in. (25 cm) in diameter

INSTRUCTIONS

Base

1. Arrange diagonally and parallel four of the 27½ in. (70 cm) strips, back side facing up. Place four more 27½ in. (70 cm) strips on top of them in the opposite diagonal direction, without intertwining them. The strips form a large diamond shape composed of nine small diamonds. To keep everything in place, put the two heavy rulers on top of them.

2. Start the weaving to the right of the bottom small diamond. Weave another 27½ in. (70 cm) strip over/under up to the top.

3. Weave a strip parallel to the first on the left side of the bottom small diamond, so as to obtain hexagons.

4. Place the final two strips on the outsides of diamonds 3 and 5. This arrangement will form a large hexagon composed of seven small hexagons.

5. Don't weave the ends of the strips, as that would disrupt the weaving of the sides.

Weaving the Sides

6. Using the folding tool, stand up the stakes on the perimeter of the large hexagon to prepare for weaving the sides.

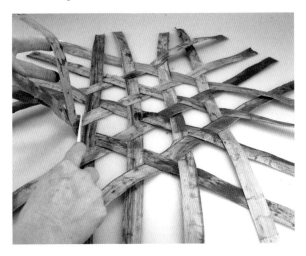

7. Place a 35½ in. (90 cm) strip at the base of the hexagon and secure the end with a clothespin. Start weaving over/under and across the stakes. Crossing the stakes helps to keep the weaver in place.

8. To finish the first round, overlap by 1¼ in. (3 cm) the start and end of the strip behind a stake. This step can be a little tricky and requires patience.

9. Continue to weave the two other strips in the same manner to assemble your basket.

10. Fold down the diagonal strips to the inside of the basket (for those that are on the outside) and to the outside of the basket (for those that are on the inside), over the third horizontal strip. Cut them ¾ in. (2 cm) from the edge.

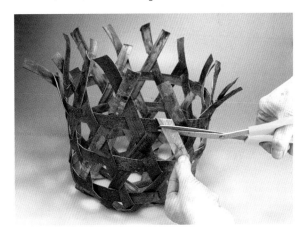

Border

11. On the inside of the basket place a strip 35½ in. (90 cm) long and ¾ in. (2 cm) wide, and hold it in place with clothespins.

15. Tie off the end of the twine to finish the border.

Decoration

16. To decorate the basket, slide the 10 in. by ³⁄₁₆ in. (25 cm by 0.5 cm) strips on top of the diagonal strips forming the sides.

12. Place the second strip on the outside.

13. Cut a length of linen twine three times the circumference of the basket's border. Attach it using a buttonhole or blanket stitch around the entire circumference of the basket, spacing the stitches ⅝ in. (1.5 cm) apart.

14. Use the awl to make holes in the strips to continue the stitches at regular intervals.

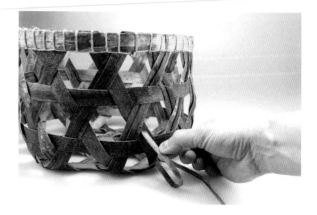

CHRISTMAS DECORATIONS

The Christmas season is a great time to decorate the home. Here are three ideas for ornaments to make with your children and share some creative time together.

PINECONE

MATERIALS

- 1 strip of willow, sweet chestnut, or hazel bark, 12 in. (30 cm) long and ⅜ in. (1 cm) wide
- 3 strips of willow, sweet chestnut, or hazel bark, 4 in. (10 cm) long and ⅜ in. (1 cm) wide
- Red and white cord
- Basic kit (see p. 10)

Size of finished ornament: 3 in. (8 cm) wide and 4¾ in. (12 cm) long

INSTRUCTIONS

1. Make the first windmill knot as explained for the windmill earrings (steps 1–4, p. 100). Leave 2⅜ in. (6 cm) at one end of the long strip.

2. Make a second knot with the front side of the second 4 in. (10 cm) strip of bark.

3. Make a third knot with the third strip. The three knots must be edge to edge, with the strips of bark extending the same length on each side.

4. Turn over the knot with the back side facing up. Cut all the strips to 2⅜ in. (6 cm) and slide all the ends into each knot.

5. Let dry for 12 hours.

6. Fold the cord in half and tie to one of the two vertical loops of the pinecone.

SNOWFLAKE

MATERIALS

- 4 strips of willow, sweet chestnut, or hazel bark, 8 in. (20 cm) long and 3/8 in. (1 cm) wide
- 2 cattail leaves
- Hole punch
- Red and white cord
- Small jingle bell
- Basic kit (see p. 10)

Size of finished ornament: 6 in. (15 cm) in diameter

INSTRUCTIONS

1. Split a cattail leaf in half lengthwise. On your work surface, place two pieces of bark in the shape of a cross and then the two others on top of that to form an eight-pointed snowflake.

2. Fold the cattail leaf in half. Place the loop around one of the bark strips; then start twining around the center (see "Techniques," p. 26).

3. Weave three to four rounds. Slide the end of the leaf into the weaving of the previous round.

4. Trim the ends of the eight strips to a point.

5. Punch a hole at the point and at the base of each strip and let dry for 12 hours.

6. Fold the cord in half and tie it to the end of a strip, including the small bell in the knot.

STAR

MATERIALS

- 5 willow stems, 6¼ in. (16 cm)
- 5 small rubber bands
- 4–5 cattail leaves, split in half lengthwise
- Red and white cord
- Small jingle bell
- Basic kit (see p. 10)

Size of finished ornament: 6 in. (15 cm) high

INSTRUCTIONS

1. Bind together four wicker stems with the rubber bands to form the letter W, as shown in the photo. Note that each stem is identified with the letter A, B, C, or D.

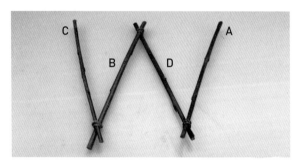

2. Pivot stem A over stem B. Pass stem C over A and under D.

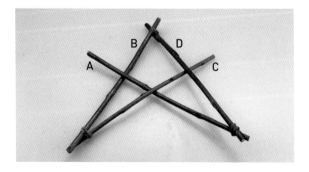

3. Place the fifth stem (E) horizontally over D and under B. Hold it in place with two rubber bands.

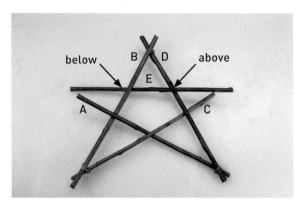

4. Catch the end of a cattail leaf in one of the rubber bands. Cover the entire point of the star with figure 8 weaving.

5. Insert the end of the leaf into the figure 8 weaving to finish filling the point. Cover the other four points in the same way.

6. Let dry for 12 hours, and then attach the red and white cord to hang the decoration, including the small bell in the cord.

ACKNOWLEDGMENTS

Several basket-weaving workshops have enabled me to enhance my work with new fibers and new techniques. Many thanks to artist and basket-maker Lois Walpole, with whom I was able to share and exchange ideas during a class, and who inspired the slippers found on page 71 of this book, freely adapted from one of her designs. I would also like to thank writer and farmer Bernard Bertrand, founder of Editions Terran, who helped me discover the world of making baskets from nature, and Michel Bonthoux, who is working on expanding the knowledge of cattail basketry in an association in the village of Jarrie, near Grenoble, and on which I loosely based the hat found on page 66.

Basket weavers are "passers-on" of their knowledge, and I am pleased to continue this tradition myself and to share with you my research and designs.

ABOUT THE AUTHOR

Basket weaving has been a large part of my professional life for more than fifteen years. I am always looking for new techniques and new fibers.

My introduction to basket weaving with rattan led me to explore many aspects of weaving because of the multiple qualities of this fiber. It is pliable, thin, and easy to dye, and it takes little time and space to start using it. I wrote four books about these techniques (*Vannerie en rotin*, 2007; *Vannerie d'aujourd'hui*, 2009; *Vannerie papier et rotin*, 2012; and *Vannerie créative*, 2017).

Basket weaving involves a group of techniques—some of which are very simple and others more sophisticated—that use plant fibers, but also more unexpected materials such as plastic and paper. I shared my creative ideas in two books—*Éco-vannerie* (2013) and *Vannerie dans tous ses états* (2015)—and since 2012 I have been writing articles for the magazine *Le lien créatif*, the first French magazine on basket weaving.

My curiosity has made me interested in the environment around me. My garden has become my workshop, a new creative area that I shared in *Vannerie tressée et cordée au jardin* (2016). In this book, *Creative Basket Weaving*, I highlight the use of cattail leaves, wicker, and the bark from willow and sweet chestnut in my creations.

I am so happy to be introducing children to this ancestral activity in schools. Basket weaving can also be a very good vehicle to wellness. With this in mind, I am responsible for teaching basket weaving to future occupational therapists at the ISTR in Lyon. Contact with these various audiences has given me a different, more complete approach to this technique.

I also organize workshops throughout the year in various locations (for associations, at retreats, for health professionals, at multimedia libraries, and so on). To see upcoming dates, go to larecreation@orange.fr.

To discover basket weaving in your own home, complete kits for children and adults are available on my website at www.vannerie-osier-rotin.com.

Sylvie Bégot